D1636208

DEEDS AND MISDEEDS
OF AN INDIAN TERRITORY DOCTOR

Elleta Nolte and Joyce McEntire

authorHOUSE®

AuthorHouse™
1663 Liberty Drive
Bloomington, IN 47403
www.authorhouse.com
Phone: 1-800-839-8640

First published by AuthorHouse 8/26/2009

ISBN: 978-1-4490-1411-7 (sc)

Printed in the United States of America
Bloomington, Indiana

This book is printed on acid-free paper.

To Marvin Earl Bullard: Elleta's brother and Joyce's father, who began this journey through time and history by asking, "Who is my family?"

Finished Reading 11-30-10

CONTENTS

INTRODUCTION

*History...*we are all components of history. Our deeds, however small, good or bad, fit in a jigsaw fashion into the history of the areas in which we live, or we touch, however briefly. While some of us simply drift with the currents of time, others ride the waves. These riders are doers with tales to tell woven into the fabric of a time or place, and others may want to listen. Names and dates and events tend to grow faint with age and fade away, while documents and photographs go astray, unless someone catches a point in time and records its history.

Relating the history of one man who was born more than a century-and-a-half ago began by dumping the pieces of puzzle on the table, sorting and fitting them in place, and in the end, searching for the missing parts. Only then did the real work begin. Perhaps some of those pieces should have been left unfound, but they fit together to more nearly complete the puzzle and the composite of a man whose deeds formed a part of the early history of a section of our nation.

I am Elleta Bullard Nolte, the granddaughter of Dr. Andrew Charles Bullard and Sarah Mae Mann Bullard. Andrew was born in Illinois in 1849 and lived there until 1885 when he abruptly left and settled in the Indian Territory of Oklahoma where he practiced medicine for forty-one years. In his lifetime, he established five families and fathered twenty-one children. At least.

My niece and co-writer of this history, Joyce Bullard McEntire, the great-granddaughter of Andrew and Sarah Mann, began the meticulous pursuit of the facts of their lives many years go and gradually lured me into it.

Joyce has long shared her passion for genealogy research with friends, family and more than a few strangers. Her relentless search for uncovering the mysteries of her family's past has led her to countless cemeteries, courthouses, paper archives, the Internet and correspondence with other sleuths across the United States.

Joyce was motivated by her dad, Marvin Earl Bullard, "He started me on the journey to find his family; and now, years later, maybe he's looking over my shoulder saying, 'go, you're almost there.' I feel that I have found our family."

Thanks to the this bloodhound trait in Joyce's nature, my innate love of history, and today's highly sophisticated methods of researching genealogy, we uncovered some fascinating facts regarding our family, and in particular the deeds and misdeeds of one Andrew Charles Bullard, the patriarch of the branch of our family that began in Illinois and ended in Oklahoma. As writers, we did not try and enter the mind of our protagonist; we simply related what we learned. Relying on the theories that truth is stranger than fiction and what you see is what you get, no part of our depiction is fictionalized, although a stray inference here and there may have escaped our keyboards.

We spent huge gulps of time in the libraries, county seats, and courthouses in Illinois and Oklahoma where Andrew lived. We pulled large and heavy, old and dusty books from their shelves;

then beginning with the year 1850, we sought his name, line-by-line. We followed all leads, interviewed available family descendants in out-of-the-way places, and gained immeasurable information from the Internet. We wove colorful threads into the chronicle, included documentation, family stories and rational speculations, struggled with inevitable snags, and at last settled for the scattered bits and pieces we gathered for this complex character. In the process, we gained a great deal of respect and admiration for the many researchers, genealogists, and historians who were always willing to help.

For historians, the story of Andrew is a part of the past to be preserved; for family members, it more nearly completes the circle of heritage. Readers may settle in to absorb the story's contents, look at Andrew's photograph, let it fire their imagination, and then let their feelings flow. Questions may remain at the end of the story, as it does for us, granting the readers the privilege of providing their own analysis.

A serious search in genealogy requires a great deal of patience and perseverance--even downright doggedness-- for only gradually do facts come together. Even then, we can never be certain of complete accuracy. Record keeping in the early years was sketchy; courthouses burned and destroyed irreplaceable data; families parted and memories faded. To add to the confusion, in the early days, census takers often spelled names phonetically. Dates were difficult to manage; it was not unusual for adults in the 18th and early 19th centuries to forget, or never to have known, their birth dates or other key dates. Overall, in researching and writing family history, we must be aware of the gravity and the enormity of our responsibility for the sake of the other researchers who may follow our paths. All we can do is to thoroughly seek the sources, record our findings in a clear and concise manner, reject the stories (however enticing) we cannot verify, and then hit the Print key.

Perhaps our history may serve as a suggestion to those who tinker with the thought of writing their own. Each family is unique; there has never been nor will there be another like it. Sometime, someone may want to research that uniqueness. If we scrape the bottom of the barrel of our minds, we can each write a novel. Follow the information trail; interview family members; search for the documents, photographs, and the writings of those who lived a portion of the history and are gone. Take advantage of today's marvelous power of technology to reach far back through buried treasures of key information. In doing so, keep your mind open and your humor intact. Life dishes out gifts and surprises, so you may find several saints and a scoundrel or two. But history never reveals all it knows and often leaves a cache of unsolved mysteries. The thrill is in the chase.

Elleta Nolte and Joyce McEntire

ANDREW CHARLES BULLARD
1849-1926

PART ONE

"I'll get on my horse and ride it through your office," said the young man, a son of a local farmer.

"I wouldn't do that if I were you," Dr. Bullard said, "If you do, I'll shoot you."

———————————————

These words pounded in the head of the doctor as he grabbed his hat, his coat, and his medical bag. Still carrying his gun, he ran out the back door of his office and to the home of his Uncle Andy. "I've killed a man," he said. "The fool was drunk, and I warned him, but he rode his horse right on into the office. I grabbed my gun and shot him."

Andrew fled the small town of Broughton in Hamilton County, Illinois in 1885 and hid out in the cane breaks of the Little Skillet River until his Uncle Andy brought him a horse, money, and provisions. Andrew headed his horse southwest and kept going, leaving his Illinois years and his responsibilities behind.

This story circulated during all of these subsequent years with various deviations within the Bullard families and has been retold by many of them. One account from a close family member told of the sighting of a wanted poster for Andrew at a bar at a business convention; another said a poster was sighted at yet another bar of an agricultural convention. One Bullard member noted that since most of the families have the murder charge in their minds that "where's there smoke, there's fire." James (Trip) Bullard, grandson from Andrew's fifth marriage, said he understood the "Pinkertons"[1] were chasing him.

3

Perhaps this relates to the long ago children's game called "whisper" or "gossip" where everyone sat in a circle and whispered something in the ear of the other, and when it completed the circle, the story was quite different, and perhaps more enticing than the original one.

Apparently, Andrew felt compelling reasons to leave his home state in 1885 and start over in a striking new territory. He was 36 and had lived all his years within a small area in Illinois; new opportunities were opening up all over the country. As for valid reasons to remain, he left behind a medical practice, a lengthy list of real estate for which he was indebted, his ex wife Rhoda Faulkner who had borne two of his children, his pregnant wife Sarah Mann who had borne five of his children, and Sarah Douglas, a young pregnant girl carrying his child. And, of course, there are imaginary reasons why Andrew fled his state. One speculation from a descendant is the wild guess that Andrew may have told the story himself to appear strong and fearless for some distorted reason.

Now, what lay ahead?

At this point, we leave Andrew heading out of Illinois and we linger to outline his past years to the point of his departure. We will look beneath the surface of his early years where there is much to see.

THE EARLY YEARS OF ANDREW

Andrew Charles Bullard was the eighth and last child of Stroud and Mary Jamison Bullard. Stroud was born in 1814 in North Carolina, son of Nathan and Sarah Stroud Bullard. Mary Jamison was born in 1811 in Virginia. The two married in Dublin County, North Carolina, then moved to Wayne County[2], Illinois, and settled in an area called Orchardville where Stroud farmed, as did many early settlers.

Stroud and Mary, the parents of this large brood of children, are not listed in the state census of Illinois between the years of 1850 and 1855, and it is thought the two had died. Historians cannot pinpoint the cause of their deaths; however, epidemics raged throughout the country between 1850 and 1900 when thousands died from influenza, cholera, and many from tuberculosis. This was a tragic period in the U.S. as many times deaths were so numerous they went unrecorded, and burials were often communal. Dr. George Ross, a retired history professor from the University of Illinois, who became a historian in Marion County, reported that a cholera epidemic went through the state in 1854. It wiped out entire towns and families. Many people went into a panic and buried their dead in woods and pastures and never went back to mark their graves.

Doris Bland, who lives and works in Wayne County, Illinois, surveyed all the graves in that county. Her research includes gravesites in the family plots that are on private land, pastures, woods and the regular cemeteries. She was not able to find any gravesites for Stroud and Mary Bullard.

Notably, none of their children died during this period of epidemics. In later census they were shown in various households. The State Census of 1855 listed the six-year-old Andrew Charles as residing in the household of his uncle and aunt, Elijah Bullard, 54, and his wife, Abigail, 52, in Hickory Hill Township of Wayne County, Illinois. This transition must have been difficult for the young boy, losing his parents and living apart from his seven brothers and sisters. Elijah and Abigail had three children; shown in 1855 *as* Frances, age 27; James, 24; and Joel, 15. For most of his formative years Andrew remained with this family as the State Census of 1865 shows him still living there at age sixteen. He may have attended subscription schools in which parents or guardians paid a subscription for each child. Or perhaps he attended the "common" school, for in 1825 the Illinois legislature passed the Free School Law that called for common schools in each county.

As for medical schooling in Illinois, Andrew's name is not among the list of the doctors who practiced in the 1880s. Medical schools and their archives were searched in regard to his schooling and none was found.[3]

Perhaps he simply hung out his shingle and began practicing medicine as sometimes occurred. After the Civil War in the 19th century, the medical profession was unlicensed in Illinois, and anyone who had the inclination to set himself up as a physician could do so. Individuals commonly learned medicine by apprenticeship or by reading medical books. But in 1877, Illinois passed legislation that required medical practitioners to possess degrees from approved medical schools or to take an examination. In 1880 Illinois adopted requirements that were enforced beginning in 1883[4]. In this regard, possibly Andrew practiced medicine under the "Grandfather clause." But did he meet any other requirement?

As it turns out, the 1870 U.S. Census shows the 21-year-old Andrew as living in the household of Nathan Williams, who is listed as a farmer and a medical doctor. Undoubtedly, it was there that Andrew developed an interest in the art of healing and may have assisted the doctor, and in doing so, Andrew may have qualified to practice medicine as in later years he said he had an office in Wayne County, Illinois.[5]

FIRST MARRIAGE

Andrew apparently developed another interest, as Dr. Williams was living at Four Mile Township, Long Prairie, in the southwest part of Wayne County, at house 53/52, while not far away at house 42/41, Warren and Elizabeth Faulkner lived with their young daughter Rhoda. She caught the eye of Andrew, and moving rather quickly, the two married in the home of the Faulkners on January 8, 1871[6].

The marriage of the young couple may have been doomed from the start, as four years later, during the September 1875 term of the Circuit Court Docket of Hamilton County, Illinois, Andrew filed for divorce on grounds of desertion. The solicitors for Andrew stated his case quite eloquently in the complainant (she was listed as Rhodie).

About the 8th day of January, the said Rhodie ceased living with your orator and has since refused to live and cohabit with him. He always conducted himself toward her with kindness and as a true and indulgent husband, supplied all her wants and necessities according to the best of his means and ability and suitable to his and her condition in life... now regarding her marriage relations and duties she has been guilty of extreme and repeated cruelty...a woman of great austerity of temper and frequently indulged in sallies of passion, and used toward our orator very obscene and abusive language without any provocation whatever, frequently refused to prepare your orator meals and perform such other household duties as it was incumbent upon her to perform...on numerous occasions used personal violence toward our orator which he did not feel disposed to resist or even defend himself against on account of her sex.

On June 8, 1873, she willfully deserted and absented herself without any reasonable cause for two years and upwards, persisted in separation and refused during this time without any just cause to live and cohabit with orator...that the said Rhodie Bullard who is made party defendant to this bill may be required to make full and direct answer to the same and that the said marriage...may be dissolved[7].

No mention was made of children in the proceedings; however, in the 1880 census of Wayne County, Illinois, two grandsons are listed as living in the Faulkner household, Robert Bullard, age 8, and John Bullard, age 6. This indicated by their ages that they were born to Andrew and Rhoda[8].

SECOND MARRIAGE

Andrew wasted no time in remarrying. He filed for divorce from Rhoda in September 1875, and the next month, October 15, Andrew Charles, 24, and Sarah Mae Mann, 19, were married in Hamilton County, Illinois[9]. His haste might have been due to the fact that Sarah was three months pregnant with their child. Within the next ten years, the couple had six children. As is often a tradition, four of the children were named after family members: Frank and Jacob were named after Sarah's two brothers, John after Sarah's father and a brother, and Rachel after her mother. The children of Andrew and Sarah Mann were:

Frank E, born: 4/27/1876, died: 9/7/1876, 5 mos

Jacob (Jake) Asbury, born: 11/16/1877, died: 8/14/1952, 74 yrs

Rachel, born: 12/18/1879, died: 12/9/1880, 12 mos

John, born: 11/28/1881, died: 9/16/1882, 10 mos

Ella Mae, born: 10/12/1883, died: 2/7/1884, 4 mos

Patrick, C, born: 11/7/1885, died: 1/15/1966, 81 yrs

The birth record of Jake shows his birth date and that his mother Sarah Mann stated that she had two children previously. This indicates she might have had another child between Frank and Jake, had a child before Frank, or even that Frank had a twin.

No birth records were found for the other children. Nor are they shown in the list of deaths in the county. Later, we received pictures of tombstones in the Barker Cemetery in Broughton, Illinois for infants Frank, Rachel, John and Ella Mae. Ordinarily, children this young are given modest markers; these children have tall beautifully crafted stones.

Parents of Sarah Mann were John and Rachel Barker Mann (our maternal grandparents. Rachel's parents were John Barker and Nancy Schoolcraft Barker). John and Rachel married March 14, 1848 and lived on a farm four miles south of McLeansboro in Hamilton County, Illinois. Their children, in addition to Sarah, the eldest, were Jacob, Frank, Andrew, John, Charles and Eliza.[10]

THE PLOT THICKENS

As it turned out, Andrew had several pressing problems in his personal life in 1885. He was confronted with two pregnant Sarahs, his wife Sarah Mann and the 17-year-old Sarah Douglas who was pregnant with his child.

Who was Sarah Douglas and how did their relationship begin? Sarah, her younger brother, John Smith Douglas, and two sisters, were born in White County Illinois to parents James E. Douglas and his first wife Martha Elizabeth Farris. She died in 1876 and James married Florence Lucinda Wiseman in 1877.

In the 1880 U.S. Census, James Douglas was listed as a laborer, and the family lived in the Allen precinct of Broughton, Hamilton County where Andrew and his family lived also. Andrew may have treated James since it shows on the 1880 census that he had a "disease of the eyes." It may be that Andrew had an eye problem also, a roving eye apart from his wife Sarah, for by late 1884, James' young daughter Sarah was pregnant with Andrew's child. This may have caused animosity between Sarah's family and Andrew adding to his woes and his plans to leave Illinois.

SIGNS OF DEPARTURE

A number of signs point to the month and year that Andrew left Illinois. Over a period of seven years, he bought and sold 24 parcels of land, mostly in Broughton. The first purchase was on April 16, 1877 and the last sold was on December 9, 1884. Starting on that date, fifteen foreclosures, assumptions, attachments, judgments, and/or quitclaims, were brought against Andrew and Sarah, the latter two brought against Sarah in 1888 after Andrew had left Illinois.[11]

So perhaps Andrew's money shortages started when he began selling his property in Broughton in 1883, and at the end of 1884, the situation had worsened as he was being sued for non-payment of property and other suits would follow. For this reason we can determine the approximate date of his departure from Illinois. He sold the last piece of property on December 9, 1884; he received the first judgment on that date.

Another significant find was the discovery in the estate box of Andrew's father-in-law, John Mann, in the courthouse in McLeansboro, three handwritten bills and receipts for medical treatment, signed by A. C. Bullard and given to John Mann for collection.[12] These verify that he did practice medicine in Illinois and seemingly indicates the date of his departure; otherwise he would have collected the money. These are:

> Mr. Joseph, Pay John Mann $6.00 for treatment of wife and daughter. Respectfully, A.C. Bullard, 12-20-1884

> Mr. James Rose, Pay to John Mann $2.50 two dollars and fifty cents and this shall be your clear receipt in full, A.C. Bullard

> Mr. Emanuel Maberry pay to John Mann $6.00 six dollars and this shall be your receipt in full, A. C. Bullard

These statements (a handwriting analyst stated, in his opinion, they were written in haste) seem to show that Andrew is leaving or has left Illinois and John was to collect these monies for him. This also may indicate that he was on good terms with his father-in-law when he left. In regard to his medical practice, Andrew's income may have been down because of competition as other doctors settled in the area.

Andrew left Broughton Illinois in late January or early February 1885 but not before he impregnated his wife Sarah Mann, for their last child, Patrick, was born November 7, 1885, well after Andrew left.

It may be that Sarah knew that her husband was leaving if her father, John Mann, had received the medical receipts for him to collect (unless he received them after Andrew left). Possibly he told his wife that he would send for her or return for her. Or perhaps he knew that the girl Sarah would follow him to Oklahoma, and he said nothing to his wife regarding his plans. Although, since Broughton was a small community, possibly some of the townspeople knew of the girl Sarah's pregnancy, including Andrew's wife Sarah. There is no way to know this.

Did the young doctor plan his departure as the facts indicate? And the matter of the murder remains. Did that occur? What happened to his wife Sarah and their two sons, Jake and Patrick, who were left behind in Illinois? Where did life lead them? Did their father simply ride out of their lives and not look back? And the young girl Sarah Douglas....

Sarah Douglas, then eighteen, left Broughton sometime in 1885 and traveled to Oklahoma with her younger brother John, who was seventeen. This is a reasonable assumption since it would be a rarity for a young pregnant girl to travel alone that great a distance at that period in time. It may be that Sarah had little choice in leaving, for often in those early years if a young woman became pregnant while living at home, she was scorned by family and friends and was sometimes forced to leave in disgrace and move to an area where she was not known. Sarah's mother had died and her father had married a younger woman, and the children did not get along with their stepmother, according to Allen Douglas, a member of the Douglas family. He also said that Andrew was influential in John's coming to the

Indian Territory. At any rate, no Douglas relatives are listed on the 1880 U.S. census for the Indian Territory, so the apparent reason she came there was Andrew. In all probability Sarah and her brother John rode the Missouri, Kansas and Texas Railroad (MKT, or the "Katy") that passed through Eufaula.[13]

To continue the saga of Andrew Charles, we leave Sarah Douglas and her brother John waiting in Eufaula at the train station and go with Andrew heading some 600 miles southwest to his chosen destination of Bullard, Texas, where it was said that he had relatives.

PART TWO

A rider on horseback can travel 20-30 miles per day. Family stories indicate that Andrew traveled this method. If so, he would had carried provisions, a medical bag and other articles, so allowing him 20 plus miles per day, he would have reached his chosen destination of Bullard, Texas (where he had relatives) in about a month, depending on his route taken.

According to family accounts, the route he followed was called the Outlaw Trail. Andrew Lewis Bullard, son of Andrew, stated the trail crossed the Indian Territory at the sandy bottom of the Canadian River where the Eufaula dam is located. At this point it was a direct line to Bullard, TX.[14]

The town of Bullard, located twelve miles south of Tyler in southern Smith County Texas, an area once occupied by Caddo Indians. The first post office was named Etna in 1867, renamed Hewsville in 1881, and Bullard in 1883. When the Kansas and Gulf Short Line Railroad arrived in 1884, the community became a shipping point for cotton, vegetables, and fruits.[15] Clearly, the town held a lot of promise to new enterprises and new settlers-- ideally a new beginning for a physician in 1885.

Ideally, yes, but not necessarily for Andrew, for he did not remain long in Bullard. He became involved in a fight with a man and "cut him up."[16] _Andrew may have made a quick decision at this time to head directly north to the Indian Territory in Oklahoma, a portion of land the government set aside in the early 1800s for Native Americans. It was a favorite retreat for lawbreakers, as law enforcement had not been fully established.

What was the Indian Territory of Oklahoma like in 1885 when the newcomer arrived there?

It was like no other place.

The land now known as Oklahoma was acquired by the United States in 1803 in the Louisiana Purchase. In 1830, President Andrew Jackson signed the Indian Removal Act that forced all Indians east of the Mississippi to leave their homes and relocate in eastern Oklahoma, in a portion of land designated as Indian Territory. Over a period of three years, thousands of Indians set out on foot with shortages of wagons, horses, blankets, and food to reach their assigned area. Many of the Indians died and were buried along the way. Five of the tribes, Choctaw, Chickasaw, Cherokee, Creek and Seminole became known as the Five Civilized Tribes because of their advanced systems of government, education and law enforcement. These tribes settled in the Indian Territory, where the tribes established territorial boundaries in self-governing national domains. Each tribe had its own "nation" and capital.[17] The census of the Choctaw Nation taken in 1885 when Andrew arrived, listed 12,816 Indians, 427 intermarried whites and 38 Negroes, making a total of 13,281 citizens.[18] When Andrew arrived, he settled within the southeast corner of the Choctaw Nation, in the small town of Brooken in Haskell County.[19]

Thus, in a dramatic lifestyle change after approximately the first half of his life, Andrew had left the quiet orderly setting of a typically small community in Illinois to live in an raucous unsettled place with unfamiliar types of people and cultures. Once there, he may have felt he was free of Illinois for a time, but two items of responsibility followed him to Oklahoma.

THIRD MARRIAGE

The young pregnant Sarah Douglas arrived in the Indian Territory sometime after Andrew reached there in 1885. They had their first child, Nellie Alice, the same year.[20]

Within the next year, 1886, Sarah Mann brought their nine-year-old son Jake to Andrew. With her also was their young son Patrick who was born the year before. Apparently Sarah had arrived in Eufaula on the train and then rented a buggy to travel to Brooken.[21]

At this point in the story, we wondered if he left Illinois on good terms with his wife Sarah Mann, and that she understood that when he settled in Oklahoma she would come and live there with him. Perhaps when she arrived the next year with their two sons, she expected to stay, only to discover he was living with another woman and their child.

The period of separation had undoubtedly been a traumatic one for Sarah Mann, for not only had she faced the many charges of land foreclosures alone in Illinois, she had suffered the terrible tragedy of losing her father, John Mann, who was brutally murdered February 19, 1886. After this occurrence, Sarah and her two brothers, Jake Mann and John Mann, left Illinois and went to Paragould, Arkansas in June 1886.[22] Now, after leaving her son Jake with his father, Sarah and her son Patrick returned to Arkansas and Andrew carried on his relationship with Sarah Douglas. (Thorough research did not uncover any divorce document for Andrew and Sarah Mann, nor could a marriage certificate be found for Andrew and Sarah Douglas.) [23] In later census' Sarah stated she was a widow.

ANDREW'S MEDICAL PRACTICE

After Andrew arrived in the Indian Territory, he resumed his practice of medicine in Brooken. There didn't seem to be any testing for qualifications to practice medicine in the Indian Territory at that time, though it has been said that the Indians did have some sort of provisions for excluding "quacks" they could identify. At statehood in 1907, provisions were made to conduct examinations for licensures; however, latitude was sometimes given to those who had a reputation for some degree of competence under the "grandfather clause." After 1908, there was a requirement that a new applicant had to be a graduate of a recognized medical school.[24] Polk's Medical Register & Directory of North America lists Andrew as practicing medicine from 1890 to 1902 in Brooken.[25]

Andrew's name is also listed with three other physicians in an undated Medical and Surgical publication for Indian Territory.[26] And in another document by D.C. Gideon in a 1901 publication for Indian Territory, states that Andrew was practicing in Brooken, arriving there in 1885.[27]

Andrew next practiced medicine in Whitefield before statehood, according to a list printed "Oklahoma Indian Territory, by Ted Bryan Hall (undated)." The publication states, "Although a number of native Choctaws were graduated from medical colleges of recognized standing during the pre-statehood period, apparently none of them chose to settle in Whitefield; the doctors who came here were white men." The publication states that Andrew received Permit No. 522 in 1892.[28]

Andrew's final move was to Quinton in Pittsburg County where his medical office was located over a drug store. The American Medical Association in its Medical Directory states his license was 1905 in Quinton District 12 in 1906, and he was grandfathered in as he was in practice before statehood in 1907. Another memorandum states that in information from Dr. John Worth Gray on February 8, 1915 that Andrew was a "non grad." [29]

OUTLAWS IN INDIAN TERRITORY

After the Indian removal to the Territory in Oklahoma in 1830, it became an outlaw paradise, as there was no law to extradite anyone for crimes in another state or territory. The outlaws roamed freely throughout the area robbing banks and trains and stealing horses and cattle. The countryside offered prime hiding places in the rocks, caves, and trees of what came to be known as Robbers Cave near present day Wilburton in the scenic hilly woodlands of the San Bois mountains of southeastern Oklahoma (today a state park). The most notorious of the outlaws included Frank and Jesse James, the Youngers, the Daltons, Bill Doolin, Ned Christie, and Sam Starr. Belle Starr, the "Bandit Queen," was the most well known of the women outlaws, and in later years, she became the subject of innumerable publications and two movies.

While the Indians had their own tribal courts and police, they had no jurisdiction over cases involving non–Indians, including the outlaws holed up there. That brand of justice belonged to the federal court established in Fort Smith, Arkansas by Congress and presided over by Judge Isaac C. Parker, who sent deputy marshals into Indian Territory to find and arrest the outlaws. Parker ruled from 1875 to 1896 with a strict brand of justice and was known as "the hanging judge" because of the many men he sent to the gallows. In 1896, Congress relieved Judge Parker of his jurisdiction of the U.S. court over the Territory. Two months later he died.[30]

ANDREW AND THE OUTLAWS

From many family stories we know that Andrew had a reputation for ministering "shot up outlaws" somewhere in hiding. Riders came on horseback in the dark of the night to his house, blindfolded the doctor and took him away. He would sometimes be gone for two-three days, and they would bring him back in the same manner. No one knew where he had gone, and he wasn't at liberty to say because he had been giving medical treatment to outlaws, and he could not divulge any information for fear of retribution.

One family story included a trip to see 'Uncle Andy.' Albert (Uel) McLain states "He gave us instructions that if we heard a knock on the door to not be alarmed, that he was sometimes called to take care of gunshot wounds for outlaws. He was called to set a young boy's arm and we went with him to his office. He told us about some of the outlaws he had doctored and said, "Since you don't live here you would not know anyone here but me and I am so old now I don't care anymore...most all are gone anyway." He told us he had doctored Belle Starr, the James Gang and others, and how he would be awakened by an outlaw, be blindfolded and taken to whoever he was to tend. He was told to never tell anyone about this or who he thought he saw, that he was always watched and so was his family, that they would be taken care of and no harm would come to them, but if anyone told, they would be killed."[31]

One of Andrew's granddaughters, Maudie Bullard, (Elleta's sister), who lived in Quinton until 1913 remembered, "Grandpa treated the outlaws. They would come get him, blindfold him and take him far out somewhere to treat one of their men. He would stay several days and they'd bring him back, and pay him in silver dollars."

At one time, Belle Starr lived in the same vicinity of Whitefield in the Choctaw Nation, as did Andrew and Sarah Douglas. It may have been about this time that according to a close family member, "Belle Starr came to the doctor's house one night to get some medicine, and he told her he was eating supper, so Belle came in and ate with him. Another time the outlaws asked if he knew a certain song and he said yes. They asked if he could whistle it, and he answered yes, so they told him to start out and when he got to a certain spot on the road he was to start whistling and almost at once a person would appear to get him.[32]

In 1882, Judge Isaac Parker sentenced Belle and her husband Sam Starr to federal prison for horse theft. They were released in 1883, and Belle returned to her home in Younger Bend in Eufaula. One wintry day in February 1889, on her 41st birthday, Belle was ambushed on a lonely road and shot to death. Her killer was never found.

A surprising bit of information appeared in the Dallas Morning News edition May 7, 1933, regarding Andrew and

Belle Starr. It was taken from articles written by Belle Starr's granddaughter, Flossie and titled "The Story of my Grandmother, Belle Starr."

> Pearl, (Belle Starr's daughter) at this time (1886) was 17 and in love with a young man two years her senior, a part Cherokee from one of the best families. The young fellows in that community were nice looking, they dressed well, they had average educations and most of them were excellent horsemen. About the only objection Belle could have to Pearl's suitor was that he was a poor boy, but she openly fought the affair. Her consuming desire was for Pearl to marry a rich man "a man with at least $25,000." So, my mother told me, she and my father went to old Doc Bullard, who married the young people of the community, and were married secretly.

By 1894, Andrew had neared a full decade in the tough and tumultuous Indian Territory in Oklahoma, administrating medical practice to people of all classes and cultures. He and Sarah Douglas had six children at this point in their lives, and at age 28 she awaited the arrival of her seventh one. Children of Andrew and Sarah Douglas:

> Nellie Alice, born: 1885, died: 1966
> Andrew Lewis, born: 1886, died: 1888
> Granville Aubrey, born: 1888, died: 1967
> James Aud, born: 1889, died: 1937
> Lidda E, born: 1890, died: 1892
> Gil L., born: 1892, died: 1892
> B.H., born: 1894, died: 1894

Sarah Douglas died four days after the birth and death of her son, B.H.

FOURTH MARRIAGE

Following his usual pattern, Andrew rushed into marriage, this time with a very young Choctaw girl. Sarah died in January 1894, and the following June 21, Andrew, now 45, married 15-year-old Villa Mae Herron who was born in February, 1879 in Sans Bois County near Brooken. She is listed on the Choctaw Census Card as Villey M. Bullard, one-half Choctaw, 2954 Roll Number, Brooken Post Office. Villa and Andrew married under Choctaw law; the tribal license cost $100. Three children were born to Andrew and Villa:

Pocahontas, born: December 28, 1897, died: circ 1909

Lu Orenia, born: August 2, 1900, died: January 23, 1974

Andrew Lewis, born: May 18, 1903

(The first son of Andrew and Sarah Douglas was named Andrew Lewis; he lived two years. This same name was given to his son with Villa in his fourth marriage. Perhaps Andrew had a specific desire for one of his children to have his name. Ironically, Andrew Lewis, Sr. and Andrew Lewis, Jr. (whom his grandfather Andrew delivered May 30, 1925) went by Lewis during their lifetimes, and not Andrew.)

During the nineteenth century, the Choctaw society institutionalized intermarriage in its laws by giving white men married to Indian women the privileges of tribal citizenship and privileges. Although many couples married for love, this was a way to wealth for white men as it included access to and control over the resources of the Indian Territory.[33] Thus, after living in the Choctaw Nation for 17 years, and eight years after his marriage to Villa, Andrew applied under oath for enrollment as a citizen by intermarriage of the Choctaw Nation.

In the Examination by the Commission on December 22, 1902, when asked how old he was, Andrew replied, "Well, I am not just sure, just about 48." (Born in 1949, he would have been 53.) He stated he had been married twice, to Sarah Mann and Sarah Douglas, neglecting to mention his first marriage to Rhoda Faulkner. Asked if there had been a separation between he and Villa of any kind whatsoever, Andrew replied: "No sir, well, she got mad about four years ago and went away and stayed three or four weeks and came back. There was no separation." The membership (roll # 653) was granted January 4, 1904.[34]

But this marriage ended in divorce also though no date is learned. Reference is made to the divorce, however, in a May 28,1990 letter from LaVern Upton Pine, daughter of Lu Orenia and granddaughter of Villa and Andrew, written to Joyce McEntire.

> Regarding the divorce so the story goes, Andrew told Villa he was going to divorce her but he would not take the children or the property if she would not contest it in court. She believed him and therefore,

did not go to court. The judge sent a law person and took the girls, my mother (Lu Orenia) and Pocahontas. He could not take Uncle Lewis as he was nursing, but the judge told her that as soon as he was weaned she was to give him up also. At that time, Villa left Indian Territory and went to Illinois where she and Uncle Lewis lived until he was eighteen. When Villa returned, she lived in or near Quinton and Stuart Oklahoma where she is buried. In the years following the divorce, Andrew sold all the Indian land he got from Villa except for Lewis' land. Later, Lewis bought most of his family's land allotments. (Regarding Pocahontas, when she was about the age of 12, fell off a building and onto a fence. She received an infection from the wound and died.)

FIFTH MARRIAGE

One more marriage remains in the story. It is uncertain when Andrew and Eula Kate Conklin (or Coglin) married, but they are listed on the 1910 census record. (Eula Kate was a nurse; maybe worked in his office.) The age shown on the census for Andrew was 55 (he was 61), for Eula Kate, 32. Their children shown in the census are Jessie M, born about 1906 and Frankie, born about 1909. Another son, James Herman was born in 1911. Eula Kate filed for divorce in October 1918. In the contract between the two regarding settlement of property rights and other issues, it gave the children the right to visit and remain with Andrew a reasonable time; the parents were not to prejudice the children against each other; and if the children were sick, Eula Kate was to advise Andrew by wire. [35]

Eight years after their divorce, on July 14, 1926, the Quinton Times, the Pittsburg County newspaper, printed on its front page that "Dr. A.C. Bullard, a pioneer practitioner in this section, died suddenly at his home...he had been downtown the day before as he walked about the street and seemed to be almost in his usual health, complaining only of weakness...he practiced medicine up to the time of his last illness." He died of myocarditis at the age of 77.

ANDREW'S LAST WILL

In Andrew's last will and testament dated June 14, 1926, one month before his death, he designated Mrs. Minnie F. Shed as executrix. He willed her Lots 1-6 of Block 82 that included his home in Quinton. He gave, bequeathed and devised the reminder of his property, both personal and real, to ten of his children: Robert W. Bullard, Jacob A. Bullard, Patrick. Bullard, Nellie Walls, Granville A. Bullard, James A. Bullard, Lu Orenia Upton, Andrew L. Bullard, Jessie M. Egerston and James H. Bullard. The will was signed by A.C. Bullard and three witnesses, H. N. Pridgen, Jack Milam, and H. D. Goodale, all of Quinton.[36]

In the Petition for Probate of Will, Mrs. Shed requests the will of A. C. Bullard be admitted to probate. The petition states that the deceased left property in the county of Pittsburg, State of Oklahoma; that the general character, description and probable value of which are about as follows: Real property of the value of about $500.00, personal property consisting principally of notes and accounts of the probable value of $500.00.[37]

The Return was contested in the matter of the estate by two of Andrew's heirs, James A. Bullard and Jacob A. Bullard on July 3, 1928 at the courthouse in McAlester. They filed their protest against the probate of the will on the grounds that A. C. Bullard was incompetent to execute a will on account of his physical and mental condition and undue influence exerted by Minnie F. Shed.

In Court Testimony in the Matter of the Estate of A.C. Bullard, on Aug 17, 1926, Mrs. Shed, in answer to questions of the attorneys, stated she had known Dr. Bullard for nine years, "He lived with us (she and her husband, James M. Shed) for seven years, paid up pretty good, yes, paid his board…He wanted me to take care of him until he died; his folks wouldn't do it; he just made the place over to me… He had been sick for about three weeks prior to his death."

In the sworn testimony of the three witnesses, H. N. Pridgen, Jack Milam and H. D. Goodale, they stated that Dr. Bullard had sent for them to come to his house and witness his signature. They said the doctor appeared to be of sound mind and memory and that he was not laboring under any undue influence, fraud, duress of any sort.[38]

Apparently, the two heirs' contest was discredited, for Mrs. Shed filed a Petition to Sell Real Estate, (the petition was undated but her signature was notarized on April 21, 1928). The petition showed that the value of the personal property was about $485.00, notes and book accounts about $50.00. The debts, expenses, taxes, charges of administration accrued and becoming due, was the sum of about $699.00. Mrs. Shed noted "There is no property belonging to the estate of said deceased in the hands of your petitioner with which pay the funeral expenses, the debts or expenses of the administration."[39]

On June 20, Mrs. Shed filed a Notice of Hearing Return of Sale of Real and Personal Estate. According to the information signed by S.F. Brown, County Judge of Pittsburg County, "She (Mrs. Shed) returned and presented for confirmation, and filed in this court, her return of the sale of all the property of said deceased…. said personal property was sold for $10.00 and said real estate for $300.00."[40]

After practicing medicine in the Indian Territory for 41 years and having owned land and property for many years, Andrew died with, at best, a minimal estate. We found many entries of his buying/selling property in the land records of McAlister, Pittsburg County, Oklahoma. Close family sources indicate that in the early days of Quinton, Andrew owned most of the south side of the town. He and two other men bought lots and sold them to settlers to help establish the town. At one time, the Randall and Bullard Addition was a part of Quinton, at least as early as 1913.

And his children…Andrew died relatively alone…as Mrs. Shed stated in her court testimony, "He wanted us to take care of him until he died; his folks wouldn't do it."

TRAITS OF ANDREW

From bits and pieces of description, we learn still more about Andrew Charles. He was listed once as belonging to the Methodist Church in Whitefield. He was also listed as a "valued representative of the Independent Order of Odd Fellows." As for politics, he was a "die hard" Republican. Family stories relate that once when his party lost the election, he strapped on his gun and remarked that he was going to clean up on the Democrats that made a habit of sitting on the streets.

One story that survived many years was that Andrew left a lake on a mountaintop in the area of Tucker's Knob, just outside of Kinta, Oklahoma. Supposedly a sign posted at the lake stated that "If a Bullard, you may fish in the lake free." Coweta Brown, Andrew's granddaughter and daughter of Granville, son of Andrew and Sarah Douglas, remembered that her parents lived beyond the lake and walked across the spillway when no water was running.

In the course of many years, Andrew Charles Bullard was apparently known as a good doctor in an area where many people knew him. Dr. Bright, who practiced medicine in Wayne City, Illinois, said he practiced with Dr. Bullard in Oklahoma. He said, "Andy was a good doctor and took a lot of patients given up on."

Kenneth Gene Oliver remembered that his dad, Jasper Marion Oliver, a blacksmith in Quinton, spoke of Dr. Bullard several times, "He said he was tough and once 'cut a man up' in a disagreement in Quinton, and after everything settled down, Dr. Bullard sewed up the man's wounds. The doctor was respected for his medical knowledge, but someone not to be taken lightly. It was not a good idea to ask questions of whites in the Indian Nation."

PERSONAL FAMILY NOTES

Andrew's grandson, Marvin Earl Bullard (son of Jake and Ethel Bullard and father of Joyce) remembered his grandfather well and always with warmth, respect and admiration. Marvin used to accompany him on his rounds, " He told me he'd make me a doctor. I remember he always wore a stiff collar with a tie," said Marvin. "His house was big with a gallery down the middle where a lot of children played and Grandpa would shoo the children away, saying, 'Take care, take care.'"

Marvin remembered that his grandfather made his rounds in a surrey pulled by two gray horses named Bob and Floppy (for one ear that refused to stand straight). He bought a car, which he learned to drive but had trouble parking. When he arrived at his office, he would simply run the car into the hitching post until it died. The solution was to hire a driver, a man named Russell to drive him on his rounds.

Jake and Ethel settled in Quinton not long after their marriage in 1896 to 1913 when they moved to Texas with their four children. I am certain that the doctor delivered some if not all of their children born there. Birth certificates were not produced in Indian Territory before 1900. After Oklahoma became a state in 1907, it didn't provide for birth certificates for another two years, didn't get around to providing certificates until about 1915, and didn't really enforce it until 1920, at least in Pittsburg County.[41]

Maudie Bullard, daughter of Jake from Andrew's marriage to Sarah Mann, described him as "not tall, but heavy, with blazing dark eyes, dark hair and wide long mustache. Though he had a sense of humor, he often looked fierce, and I was scared of him, yet I loved him. I was thirteen when my family left Quinton, and I knew that we would all die without Grandpa to take care of us. Once he came to see me when I was sick, and I said, 'Grandpa, my head hurts, and he said, 'Hell, my head hurts too.'"

Ethel Omega Burns Bullard (Elleta's mother) often mentioned how "very good Grandpa was to me." She also said that Jake (my father) was "cuffed around" as a child, and I feel this is true. I remember my father as mild mannered, and I never saw him display any temper; however, he never showed any interest or affection for any of us six children who grew to adulthood; he simply ignored us. Perhaps since he never received love or attention in all his early years, it was hard to give any, and perhaps that was true of his father, Andrew Charles. To my knowledge, my father never received any schooling; he had a sharp mind, learned to read on his own and became an avid reader, but his writing and speaking skills suffered. On the other hand, perhaps Andrew had little formal schooling other than what he learned on his own and perhaps this was typical of the times in early Illinois and the Indian Nation in Oklahoma.

And the murder charge? As colorful as it might be, in a careful scrutiny of the court records of Hamilton and Wayne Counties where Andrew lived in Illinois, we found no murder charge for him.[42] We did find that he and father-in-law John Mann might have caroused together for in February 1880 they were both arrested for selling whiskey. Andrew was arrested five other times for selling alcohol, from February 1879 to September 1881.

No murder charge…and yet, back to the whisper/gossip game, Andrew could have committed a crime in another Illinois county away from Hamilton or Wayne. He could have hidden in the cane breaks of the Little Skillet River. Its fork rises in northeastern Marion County and flows generally southeastwardly through Clay, Wayne, Hamilton and White Counties. He could even have committed the crime on the way out of Illinois. Yet, if one searched the entire records of the counties in the whole state of Illinois for a murder rap, what would that prove? That deeds of violence can be hidden? That the crime did not occur? After a hundred and a quarter years, it remains a very cold case.

PART THREE

Many of us like a good mystery, a story of a happening that piques our interest and at first cannot be understood or explained. Usually, however, by the last chapter, we are ready for the solution. In fiction, it usually appears. In reality, not necessarily.

This is mainly the story of Andrew Charles Bullard, our grandfather. But what of our paternal grandmother, Sarah Mae Mann Bullard, Andrew's second wife--what happened to her? And Patrick, their last child—where did life lead him? Acting on the theory that you can run but you can't hide, at least forever, we began the search for Sarah and Patrick.

We last left Sarah Mann as she brought her two sons, Jake and Patrick, to their father Andrew in the Indian Territory, probably in mid-June 1886. She left Jake and returned with Patrick to Paragold in Green County, Arkansas. She and her two brothers, Jake and John Mann, went there after the murder of their father, John Mann, the previous February. Sarah had faced alone the foreclosures of her and Andrew's properties after he left in early 1885. Perhaps Sarah was left without adequate money or income.

Our search for Sarah and Patrick eventually led to Evansville, Vanderburgh County, Pigeon Township in Indiana. Evansville was a town of 60,000 people at that time, approximately sixty miles west of Sarah's home in Broughton, Illinois. The U.S. Census of 1900 showed that she and Patrick were living in what appeared to be a large rooming house at Number 262, with 25 roomers, many working for the Southern Railroad in various capacities. [43] (In this census, they are given the name

Bullen instead of Bullard.) Sarah was shown as head of the household, indicating she was in charge of the care of the house or perhaps she was a domestic there. The census stated that she was widowed and was born in 1874, neither statement correct. Her husband Andrew was very much alive and Sarah chopped 18 years off her age; she married in 1875. But correctly, her son Patrick's age is shown as fourteen, and he was attending school.

Sarah did not appear in the 1910 U.S. Census, but appeared in the 1920 Census as living in Meridian, Ward 1, Lauderdale County, Mississippi, as well as in the 1918-1919-city directory of Meridian, Mississippi as living at 2008 9th Street. The record also shows that she has three roomers, J.M. Creed and his wife Mary, and a Billie Barnes. The clue that led to her location was found in an obituary of one of her brothers, Andrew Mann, who died in 1931 in which it is stated that his sister, Sarah Bullard, lived in Meridian, Mississippi.

In the 1930 U.S. Census, Sarah lived in Laurel, Jones County, Mississippi, at 107 Pine Street, and she was head of a household. Sarah died eight years later after a year's illness, according to her obituary dated June 18, 1938, and was a "beloved resident of Pine Street." It further stated that she was born in McLeansboro, Illinois, she was a widow, a domestic, and her father was John Mann. Her birth date was shown as April 23, 1865. (She was born in 1856.) She appeared in genealogy records of the Laurel Mississippi library as being buried in the Hickory Grove Cemetery.[44]

As for Patrick, he does not appear as Patrick again. But obituaries can produce living facts. On the obituary for Sarah is the information that she has one son, B.E. Bullard. With this knowledge, we began searching for her son by this name and found that in the 1910 U.S. Census, he was listed as living in a boarding house; he was 28, single and working for the Southern Railroad. Through a series of intense searches we learned that sometime between 1900 when he was fourteen and 1906 when he was 20, Patrick abandoned the name Patrick and assumed the name of Blake Easton. He went to work for the Southern Railway in 1906 under that name.

We also found listed in the records of Laurel Mississippi that Blake Easton Bullard and Nella May Schlager were married on January 24, 1911. They had one daughter, Dorothy.

But Nella filed for divorce from Blake in 1915 in Lauderdale County, Mississippi; the divorce was finalized in 1917. Then, the 1920 U.S. Census shows that that Blake was 33 years old and was now a locomotive engineer for the railroad. Blake's wife (his second) was Alexius and he had a stepdaughter, Dollie Mager, age seven.

Why does one change a given name? For professional and career uses? To hide from creditors? Ex-spouse? To satisfy a whim of personality? To assume a "Hollywood" style moniker? To evade a dark past, a crime? A letter dated November 8, 2008, to the Vanderburgh County Clerks Library in Evansville, stated that no crime charges were ever made against Blake or Patrick Bullard. Perhaps in some cases, people simply do not like their given names. Yet, strangely, Blake Easton usually inserted "Pat" within his name and he insisted he be called Pat.

Documents from the railroad gave us much information regarding Blake Easton Bullard. His retirement news item lists him as "Brother Blake 'Pat' E. Bullard." Beyond a doubt, Blake Easton was indeed our Patrick. In fact, a document filed on April 7, 1939 for his retirement and annuity, he stated that his father was Andy Charles Bullard and his mother was Sarah May Mann.

Finally, a clue that cinched the connection of Blake Easton. Bullard to Patrick Bullard: Blake's daughter, Dorothy, had a grandson, Charles Lindley, and we found him in the Meridian Mississippi phone book and had a conversation with him. Charles graciously gave us the information we long sought, an insight into Blake's/Patrick's character and clippings he forwarded to us:

As a child, Charles spent vacation time in the summer with his grandfather Blake. He provided well for his daughter Dorothy. He told her that if she graduated from high school, he would buy her a diamond ring. She finished and received a beautiful ring that cost $250 (this occurred during the Depression).

Blake had a penchant for gambling (as did some of his fellow workers). He would sometimes go to the firehouse and play any kind of games that they had going. With a strong eye for profit, he lent money to the men, one dollar for two.

Blake E. (Pat) Bullard retired from Southern Railroad in 1954. He had a clear 48-year record on the Southern Railway. From December 1906 when he began as fireman, until July 1954 when he retired as locomotive engineer, he was never involved in a serious accident. Blake was treasurer of the railroad fraternity that gave the Methodist Church in Laurel, to which he belonged, a large stained glass window that remains there today.

Blake "Patrick" died in the Golden Service Guest House in Lauderdale County of Mississippi of a heart condition after a long illness. Yet, more mystery…on his death certificate, it shows correctly that he was born in Illinois on November 17, 1885. It stated that his father's name and also his mother's maiden were not known. His wife Lucille gave the information. Lucille Simmons, his third wife, married Blake on November 22, 1924. She operated a beauty shop in Laurel for 35 years.

Blake was buried in the Hickory Grove Cemetery near his mother Sarah. So this mother and her son remained close. Sarah's other son Jake (Elleta's father) was living in Comanche, Oklahoma in 1938 when Sarah died. She had visited him once when he lived in Quentin in 1913. As a child, I never heard my parents mention my grandparents, Andrew and Sarah. It was not the age of communication, specifically with children.

IN CONCLUSION

The life story of Dr. Andrew Charles Bullard has taken the reader through an intriguing trail of mystery and presents a stunning study in human nature. In researching and writing this story, it occurred to us that Andrew would not conceive, nor would he believe, that a century-and-a-half after his birth, that two of his granddaughters would wish to, or dare to hang onto his coattail and follow him through the happenings and oddities of his life and tell of them. On the other hand, perhaps he would recognize that these occurrences made him a small component of the history of a section of our nation and willingly consent. Aside from that, he might have delighted in leading us in pantomime through the game of charade with its twists and turns, never quite revealing who and what he was, and in seeing his slightly bewildered granddaughters searching valiantly for the answers.

None of us can choose our parentage, only how we choose to live out our heritage. Certainly, we two researchers/writers are indebted to Andrew for our very lives; and since we're cut from the same cloth, so to speak, we have inherited in part from him our characteristics and personalities, our peculiarities of features and mannerisms. As for Andrew's misdeeds, skeletons may line the closets of many families if they wish to rattle the bones. In compensation, we can look at the long lines of Bullard offshoots, who mainly are morally good, hardworking, and honorable people.

Elleta Nolte and Joyce McEntire.

PART FOUR

Who are we? What is the origin of the surname Bullard and its variations of spellings including Buller, Bulwer, De Boulard, De Blullwarde and Bullward? This question has never been answered to the satisfaction of all without drawing on the imagination. One enticing surmise was made by Edgar J. Bullard, of Detroit, Michigan, author of *Bullard and Allied Families,*" in the 1920s, "The surname Bullard is of Norman-French origin, tracing back to the 10th century when the Norman *De Boulard* or *De Boulwarde* was carried into England by the followers of the Conqueror."

This belief seems to tie in somewhat with the views of another historian, E. M. Bullard in a booklet titled, *The Bullards of North Carolina,* in 1957. He writes: "We can be reasonably sure that we are a segment or an element of some of the tribes, cults or peoples which developed during the *Dark Ages*...the time of the Vikings, Huns, Norsemen and the Danes in western Europe. Out of these were born the Angles, Saxons, Celts, Teutons, Normans, Bretons, Welch, Irish and Scots."

This same historian suggests the Bullards migrated with the Normans to the northwest section of what is now France and assumed the name *De Bullward.* They continued their migration into England with the followers of William the Conqueror during the latter half of the 11th century.

Spencer Ardell Bullard, an eminent historian and researcher, brought us a little more up to date with his book *William and Nathan Bullard Family.* [45] In it, Spencer writes," There is considerable evidence supporting the belief that nearly all American Bullards descend from a settlement of Bullards in or near Suffolk and Norfolk Districts near London in the 15th and 16th Centuries. These Bullards are believed to have arrived in England from France with William the Conqueror in the latter part of the 11th Century."

OUR LINEAGE

Following a great deal of in-depth research, Spencer Ardell Bullard learned that the genealogy of our particular strain of Bullards has been linked to William Bullard and spouse unknown of Duplin County, North Carolina. Spencer further substantiated this by gathering together a group of Bullard relatives and conducting Y-DNA tests in search of common ancestors, starting in July 2008 and finishing in September 2008. Final analysis proved that we share a common ancestor, Nathan1 and Sarah Stroud Bullard within four to six generations, that the second, third, sixth and eighth sons of Nathan1and Sarah Stroud Bullard were our most recent common ancestors.

Family ancestral line of Elleta and Joyce is:

William Bullard and spouse unknown were listed in the 1786 State Census in Duplin County, North Carolina. William, born: about 1725 and believed to have, died: 1796-1797. He had three sons, Nathan, William, and Joshua.

Nathan Bullard, son of William Bullard, born about 1765, died in 1842. He married Sarah Stroud January 21, 1795 in Dublin County, North Carolina. Sarah, born about 1775 in Dublin County, died in 1837. [46] Their children:

Wright, born: 1797
William, born: 1800
Nathan, born: 1805
Elijah, born: 1806
Asa, born: 1806 (Asa and Elijah may have been twins)
John, born: 1810
Stroud, born: 1814
Lorenzo Dow, born: 1816
Sarah, born: 1821

It is believed that Nathan had a first wife (name unknown) in 1784 before he married Sarah Stroud in 1795. They had two children: William3 and an unnamed daughter.

Stroud Bullard, son of Nathan and Sarah Stroud Bullard was born in 1814 in North Carolina. He married Mary Jamison, born in 1811 in Virginia. They are believed to have died 1850-1855. U.S. Census of Wayne County, Illinois in 1850 listed the children:

Robert 19
Frances Marion 14
James R 12
Eliza, 10
Mary Jane, 8
Wright 6
Melissa 3
Andrew Charles 1.
Louisa Watkins, 16, (possibly a relative or servant)

<u>Andrew Charles</u>, son of Stroud and Mary Jamison Bullard, born in 1849 in Illinois. He married <u>Sarah Mae Mann</u> in 1875, born in 1856 in Illinois.

<u>Jacob Asbury Bullard</u>, son of Andrew Charles and Sarah Mae Mann, was born January 6, 1877 in Wayne County, Illinois, died August 14, 1952 in Ryan, Oklahoma. He married <u>Ethel Omega Burns</u> in 1896. She was born September 11, 1881 Henderson County, Texas and died February 11, 1954 in Marlow, Oklahoma. Their children:

Two infants: Otto and Agnes, born and died in Oklahoma before 1899

Maudie Gladys: born October 3, 1900 in Quinton, OK died May 6, 1991 in Oklahoma City, OK

Jacob Elvin: born June 6, 1903 in Quinton, OK, died April 24, 1971 in Tishoming, OK
Marvin Earl: born May 15, 1906 in Quinton, OK died December 31, 1996 in Duncan, OK

Eva Idalene: born April 14, 1910 in Quinton, OK, died November 7, 1989 in Oklahoma City, OK

Walter: born and died about 1912 at Ft. Smith, AR

Alva Charles: born October 23, 1914 in Waurika, OK, died January 9, 1997 in Las Vegas, NV

Opal Ethel: born and died in 1917 in Oklahoma

Flora Elleta: born March 18, 1919 in Waurika, OK

Verlon Myrtle: born August 6, 1922 in Oklahoma, died December 24, 1928 in Oklahoma

Marvin Earl Bullard, son of Jacob and Ethel Bullard, born May 15, 1906 in Quinton, OK. He married Opal Estelle Vanlandingham, born January 11, 1908 in Texas. Their children:

Ethel Earlene, born 1932, died few months later
Joyce Florene, born April 6, 1934
Mickey Earl, born December 4, 1938, died June 4, 2003

Joyce Bullard McEntire, daughter of Marvin Earl Bullard and Opal Vanlandingham, born April 6, 1934 in Oklahoma. She married Victor Wandel McEntire July 19, 1950, born February 25, 1932. Their children:

Victor Wandel, born December 23, 1951
Ricky Earl, born July 30, 1954
Sammy Charles, born December 15, 1955
James Darrell, born August 24, 1959
Vicki Joyce, born August 11, 1961

Elleta Bullard Nolte, daughter of Jacob and Ethel Bullard, born March 18, 1919 in Waurika, Oklahoma. She married Quenton Carl Nolte, January 27, 1944 in Pampa, Texas, born April 5, 1919 in Watkins, Iowa. Their children:

Quenton Carl, Jr., born July 24, 1945

Dale Ross, born August 31, 1947

David Charles, born November 19, 1948

Alan Ray, born July 19, 1950, died March 11, 1978

Marsha Elleta, born March 15, 1952

Dwaine Key, born November 3, 1954

Patricia Elaine, born August 31, 1958

Gary Steven, born August 18, 1960

Leigh Ann, born May 9, 1962

AND NOW:

Over a period of several years, we researched family data to the nth degree, discarded most of the hearsays we could not verify, and recorded the remainder to the best of our abilities. We sought to inform you, perhaps to challenge you, and in a mild form to entertain you. It has been an absorbing journey, but we are ready to take another path in another direction. As baseball star Yogi Berra advised, "When you come to a fork in the road, take it."

ENDNOTES

[1] Wikipedia Encyclopedia: The Pinkerton agency was a private U.S. security guard and detective agency established by Allan Pinkerton in 1850. He became famous when he foiled a plot to assassinate president-elect Abraham Lincoln, who later hired Pinkerton agents for his personal security during the Civil War.

[2] Wikipedia Encyclopedia: Wayne County, Illinois was formed in 1819 out of Edwards County. It was named after General "Mad Anthony" Wayne, an officer in the Revolutionary War and Northwest Indian War.

Illinois derived its name from the native Illiniwek tribes in the area. American settlers began arriving in 1810, drawn to the heavily wooded area in the south. Later arrivals pushed up into the prairie lands in the northern part of the state. In 1881, Illinois became the 21st state to join the union.

[3] From Washington School of Medicine, archivist Paul Anderson, January 16, 1990, "Search of records of Medicine & Historical records, alumni list shows nothing found for Andrew Bullard.

St. Louis University Medical Center School of Medicine, Sally S. Ward, Registrar & Academic Record Mgr, November 13, 1989, "Records searched and nothing found for Andrew.

From St. Louis Medical Society Library, librarian Emilia V. Rogers, November 15, 1989, "No record found of Andrew ever being a member of St. Louis Medical Society."

[4] Ronald Hamowy, The Early Development of Medical Licensing in the U.S. 1875-1900, Dept of History, University of Alberta, www.mises.org/journals.

[5] The name is listed as Adam C. Bullard; no record of the name is given elsewhere during this period. Original census records indicate that Andy became Adam by the census taker. He is listed as a farmhand

that he may have been in addition to being Dr. William's helper in his medical practice.

[6] It is possible that after Andrew and Rhoda married, he worked with Dr. Sherwood Purcy in Illinois for a time. Records in Indian Territory, Oklahoma, Andrew stated that he worked under Dr. Purcy who is found in three censuses. The spelling of his name is different in each but it does show him as an MD. He is living in Belle City in Jefferson County as Pearcy; in 1870 living in Hamilton County as Piercy; then in 1880 back to Jefferson County as Pearcy. This would be due to inaccurate spelling by the census taker. Another clue to his medical training is that the 1880 census lists Andrew as a farmer and MD who is living next door to a Dr. Wheeler. He may have continued his study with Dr. Wheeler, joined him in practice, or had his own practice by that time.

[7] State of Illinois, Hamilton County, in the Circuit Court, the September Term 1875, to the Honorable Lazwell B. Tanner.

[8] Robert Bullard married Louisa Jones, and the two had seven children, Bert, Lilly, Harry, Ernest, Betty, Edna, and Lester. Robert, prominent and respected, had a nursery and plant farm. "He was freehearted, always giving vegetables and plants to others. He never talked about his father," said Fern Bullard, wife of Lester. (Letter to Joyce McEntire from Fern Bullard, March 19, 1991.) Yet, later, Fern stated that Robert visited Andrew a few times in Oklahoma. Robert is included in his will when he died in 1926. John, the second son of Andrew and Rhoda, was an epileptic and died in a mental institution. According to the Wayne County, Illinois marriage index, Rhoda married James Brown November 24, 1879. She died shortly after childbirth in Wayne County Township, Illinois.

[9] The marriage license lists Andrew as 24; born in 1849, he would have been 26. Hamilton County in which they were married was named after Alexander Hamilton, and was created in 1821 from the western part of White County. The village of Broughton Illinois began as Rectorville in 1857. The railroad missed the village, so the inhabitants went to the railroad and established Broughton after surveyor Broughton.

[10] John Mann was born in Tennessee about 1823 and came with his parents, Elijah and Nancy Hunter Mann to Illinois about 1830. In 1846 John enlisted in the U.S. Army and served in the Mexican War under Captain Lawler of Shawnee Town, Illinois. After the war, he came back to Illinois and settled on a farm of about 200 acres five miles south of McLeansboro in Hamilton County. John married Rachel Barker on March 15, 1848. Rachel was born in 1830 in Hamilton County, Illinois. Her parents were John Barker and Nancy Schoolcraft. Rachel died September 7, 1876. Shortly afterwards, John married Susan A. Tatum. They had two children, William and Julie.

But a tragedy occurred in 1886, a year after Andrew left Illinois. According to the McLeansboro Times on February 18, John Mann, Sarah's father, was ambushed and killed at Hog Creek, four miles west of Broughton while riding his horse to his daughter's farm, commonly known as the Bullard land. A week later, three brothers, George, Hardeman and Marion Schoolcraft (relatives of Rachel Mann, Sarah's mother) were arrested and charged with the described premeditated murder. Each was sentenced to 25 years in Chester Penitentiary in Randolph County, Illinois.

However, one of the brothers, James Hardeman, while a convict, swore that he alone killed John Mann after accusing him of stealing a horse from his brother ten years earlier. "He (John Mann) bitterly denied it and threatened my life…some time elapsed and I could hear threats…I became afraid and determined to revenge myself. I was young and revenge haunted me…I have learned better things since. One morning we met on the road and I shot and killed Mann…my brothers, George and Marion, knew nothing of my determination… they were in no way involved and are innocent of the crime."

These statements were made to the prison chaplain, T.M. Griffith, and in a letter December 4, 1891 to Hon John C. Edwards, McLeansboro, Illinois, Griffith explained, "I talked to all the boys, and I am quite well advised that it was no reconverted plan of action between the men, as they cell separately…if the boys are innocent, they should have speedy relief."

Letters to the governor regarding the release of George and Marion indicated the belief that James alone was guilty of the murder. Marion was pardoned in 1892 and indications are that George was released from prison also.

[11] Andrew bought the first lot in Broughton on April 16, 1877 and was still buying property on August 4, 1883, but beginning four days later, on August 8, 1883. He began selling his property, a total of five pieces of land, ending December 9, 1884. Starting on that date was a total of fifteen foreclosures, assumptions, attachments, judgments, and quitclaims, against Andrew and Sarah, the latter two brought against Sarah in 1888. One foreclosure against Sarah was an assumption at a bank in Evansville, Indiana. This list was found in county clerk records in McLeansboro, Illinois.

[12] Receipts were found in Hamilton County records in McLeansboro by Darlene Sewell.

[13] Wikipedia Encyclopedia: The Missouri-Kansas-Texas (MKT, or Katy) operated 1870-1989 and was the first railroad to enter Texas from the north. Eufaula in McIntosh County was once known as an Indian Center of the Creeks. It developed into a town after the arrival of the MKT. John Douglas went back to Illinois and married his childhood sweetheart, then returned to the Indian Territory and later moved to Oregon, where he died. Sarah's sister Mary came to Oklahoma married James Qualls and died there. Sarah's father James also came to the Indian Territory and lived for a time

[14] During the development of the Outlaw Trail that traversed from Illinois to Texas, the trail changed names and routes. The West Shawnee Trail was developed as a branch of the Shawnee Trail because the Indians levied a tax on herds that trailed through Indian Territory. The Indians also caused stampedes that resulted in cattle that the drovers could not find, and the Indians found after the herd moved on. This information from Dale Chlouber, Washington Irvin Trail Museum, in e-mail, to Joyce McEntire, October 22, 2008.

[15] Bullard, Texas, Handbook of Texas Online.

[16] A long bladed knife may have been a part of Dr. Bullard's medical

kit as he used one to mix medication. As a small boy, Marvin Earl Bullard, the doctor's grandson in Quinton Oklahoma, watched him as he mixed medication, "He would put this knife down into a bottle of stuff and put it on a little paper, then add something else and mix it altogether with his knife to make the dose of medicine for his patient."

[17] Oklahoma State History and Information, www.state.ok.us.

[18] Angie Debo, Rise and Fall of the Choctaw Republic, University of Oklahoma Press, 1961.

[19] Brooken, a small town in northwestern Haskell Co, retained a post office from 1858 to1879. It took its name from Brooken Creek. Information given by Mary T. Eufaula Memorial Library in e-mail to Joyce McEntire, August 21, 2008.

[20] Interesting items regarding Nellie and her husband, Thomas. Benjamin Walls: His parents were born in the Choctaw Nation, Indian Territory. His father, Thomas J. Walls was Deputy Marshall in the Nation in the 1880s. Thomas, himself, became a Sheriff Deputy and also a Federal Marshal. He organized the First National Bank of Poteau, Oklahoma in 1904. He secured leases and drilled in the first gas wells in the LeFlore County Gas Field in 1910, and piped the gas into Poteau. Thomas also organized and helped furnish the capital to build the first electric light plant on east side of old Indian Territory in 1906. Nellie enrolled in the Choctaw Tribe as an intermarried in 1902.

[21] Floyd and LaNell Bullard, who had a recording of a housekeeper that once worked for Andrew. Floyd was the son of Charlie Bullard, son of Elizabeth Bullard, Andrew's sister.

[22] Legal document from John Judd, Clerk of the County Court of Hamilton County, Illinois, found in the will box of John Mann in Hamilton Co to Sarah Bullard, Jake Mann and John Mann at Paragould, Green County, Arkansas, August 18, 1887, from State of Illinois, A. A. Young and Samuel Mann, administrators of the estate of John Mann and Susan A. Mann, et al, petition to sell real estate to pay debts. Documents courthouse.

[23] Victor D. Hart, researcher at the genealogy library at McAlister OK states there is no record of a divorce from neither Sarah Mann nor a marriage license for Sarah Douglas.

[24] Letter to Elleta Nolte from Thurman Shuller, M.D. Pittsburg County Genealogical & Historical Society, June 11, 1998.

[25] Polk's Medical Register & Directory of North America. Information from directories, Letter to "LaNell" from Micaela Sullivan, American Medical Association, Chicago, Illinois, August 3, 1983.

[26] This list, though undated, shows the population of Brooken as 30 and refers to the "whites and civilized Indians only." Other information includes "The Indians (in Indian Territory) have made considerable advances in civilization during the past few years, have newspapers printed in their own language, good schools and are engaged in agriculture and a few branches of manufacturing."

[27] D.C. Gideon, Indian Territory, descriptive Biographical and Genealogical, Landed Estates, County Seats, New York and Chicago, 1901.

[28] Ted Bryan Hall, Oklahoma Indian Territory, undated.

[29] At that time, whites were required to pay a small rental fee to live in the Territory. Quinton is located in Pittsburg County, Oklahoma, between the foothills of the Ozarks and the San Bois Mountains. The area was once known as "Alexander Gap," a pass in the mountains. The town was named after Martha Elizabeth Quinton, a prominent local Choctaw. She died in 1941 at the age of 115, the mother of nine children.

[30] Oklahoma's History, www.state.ok.us.

[31] "The Trip to Uncle Andy's," Uel McLain as told to Elaine McLain Tolbert (undated).

[32] Conversation between Joyce McEntire and Coweta Brown, daughter of Granville Bullard, son of Andrew and Sarah Douglas.

[33] Clara Sue Kidwell, The Choctaws in Oklahoma, University of

Oklahoma Press, Norman, Oklahoma, 2007.

[34] Application of Andrew C. Bullard for enrollment as an intermarried citizen of the Choctaw Nation, Department of the Interior, Commission to the Five Civilized Tribes, South McAlester, Indian Territory, December 22, 1902. He is listed on the census card as Choctaw, Degree 1W, 2954 roll number, Brooken Post Office.

[35] Contract between A.C. Bullard and E.K. Bullard, Quinton, Oklahoma, November 19, 1918.

[36] Last Will and Testimony of A. C Bullard, June 14, 1926.

[37] Petition for Probate of Will to the Honorable S.F.Brown, Judge of the County Court of Pittsburg County, State of Oklahoma, undated.

[38] Testimony in Matter of Estate of A. C. Bullard, August 17, 1926.

[39] Petition to Sell Real Estate, Minnie F. Shed, April 21, 1928.

[40] Notice of Hearing of Sale of Real and Personal Estate, June 20, 1928.

[41] Letter from Thurman Shuller, M.D. Pittsburg County Genealogical and Historical Society, June 11, 1998 to Elleta Nolte.

[42] Letter dated March 11, 1990 from Wayne County, Illinois Circuit Clerk Office to Joyce McEntire, "I have checked my records thoroughly and find no record for Andrew Charles Bullard," Signed: Elias W. Simpson.

[43] Wikipedia Encyclopedia. The Southern Railway was a former United States railroad. It was the product of nearly 150 predecessor lines that combined and reorganized in the 1830s, becoming the southern Railway in 1894. It was placed under control of the Norfolk Southern Corporation and was renamed Norfolk Southern Railway in 1990.

[44] E-mail on August 26, 2008 to Joyce McEntire from Susan Blakely, genealogy clerk at the Laurel Library, Mississippi.

[45] Spencer Ardell Bullard, William and Nathan Bullard Family: History

and Genealogy, Lakewood Colorado, March 2004.

[46] Parents of Sarah Stroud Bullard were Lutson and Hanna Stroud. Lutson Stroud Jr is listed as one of the Revolutionary War Solders who served in the North Carolina militia. He was wounded in one of the battles.

LaVergne, TN USA
20 September 2009
158442LV00004B/29/P